peaceful piano solos: soundtracks

a collection of 30 pieces

ISBN: 978-1-5400-8698-3

Visit Hal Leonard Online at
www.halleonard.com

Contact Us:
Hal Leonard
7777 West Bluemound Road
Milwaukee, WI 53213
Email: info@halleonard.com

In Europe contact:
Hal Leonard Europe Limited
42 Wigmore Street
Marylebone, London, W1U 2RN
Email: info@halleonardeurope.com

In Australia contact:
Hal Leonard Australia Pty. Ltd.
4 Lentara Court
Cheltenham, Victoria, 3192 Australia
Email: info@halleonard.com.au

American Beauty

from the DreamWorks Major Motion Picture *American Beauty*

By Thomas Newman

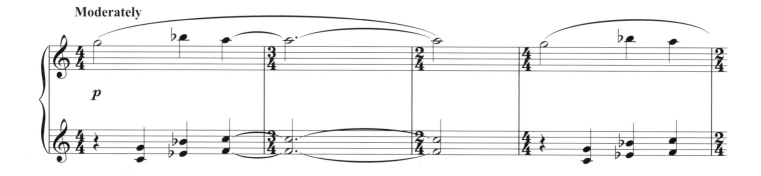

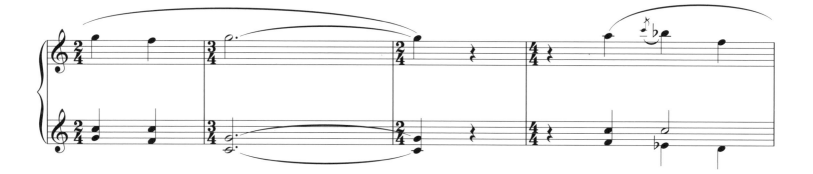

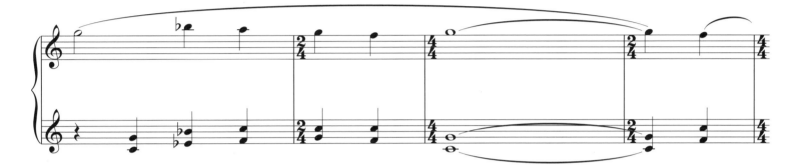

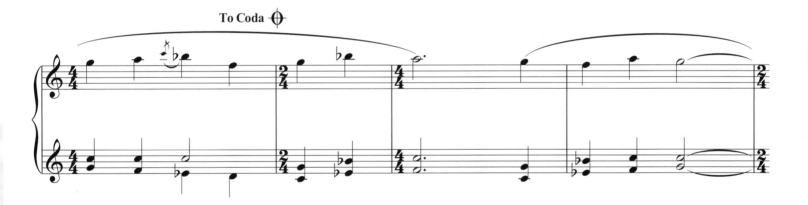

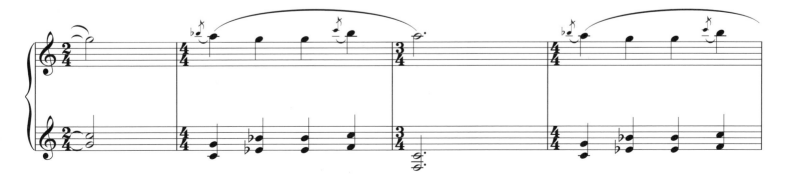

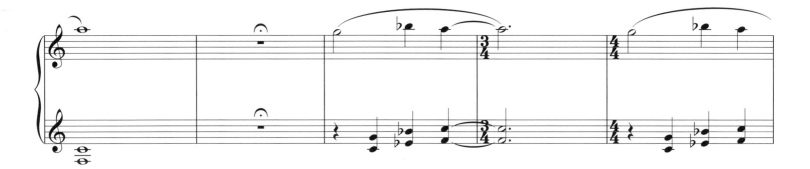

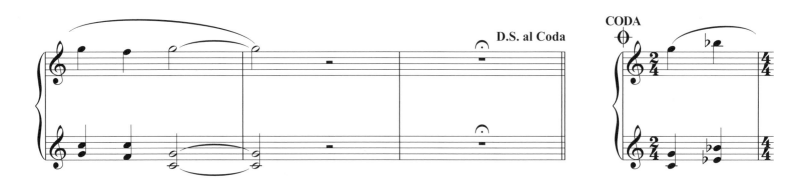

D.S. al Coda

CODA

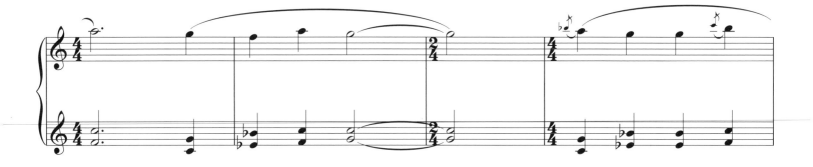

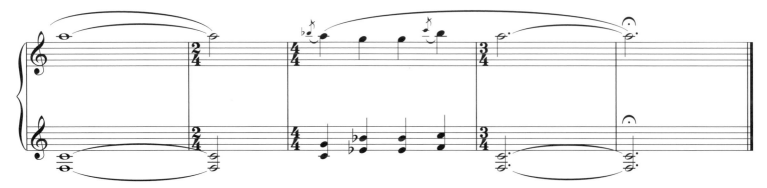

Balcony Scene

from the Twentieth Century Fox Motion Picture *Romeo + Juliet*

Words and Music by Nellee Hooper, Marius Devries,
Craig Armstrong, Tim Atack and Desree Weekes

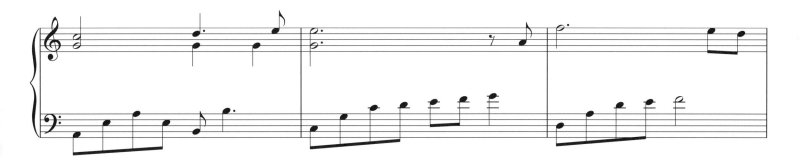

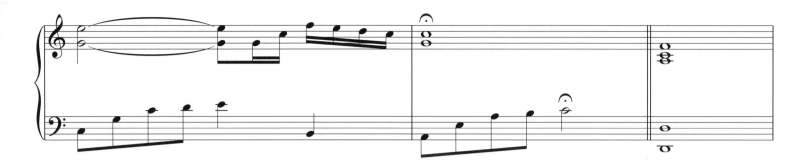

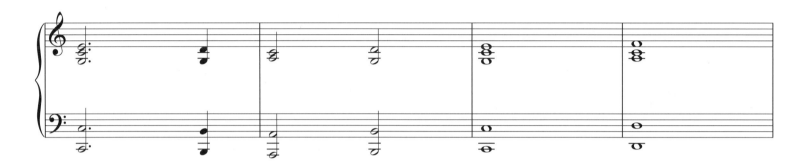

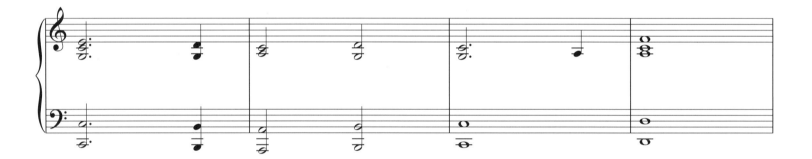

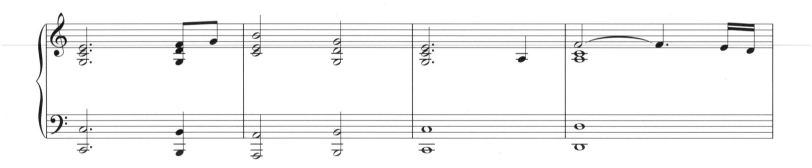

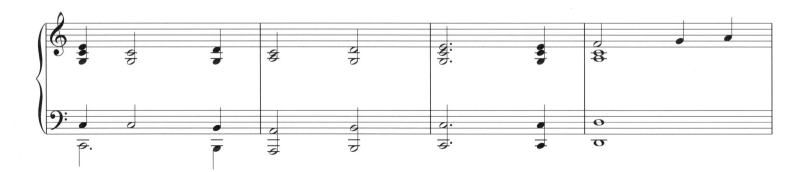

8

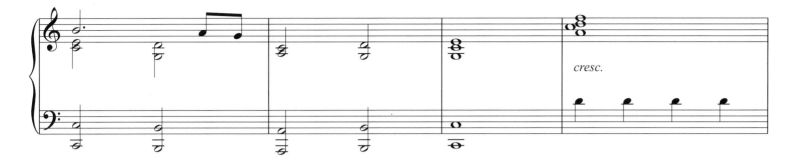

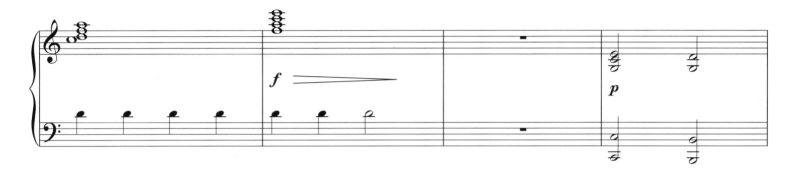

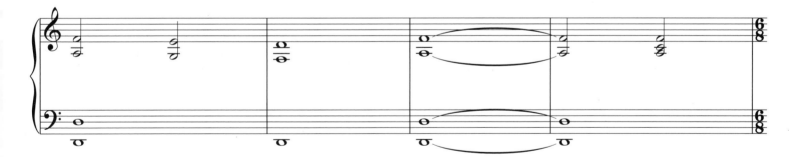

9

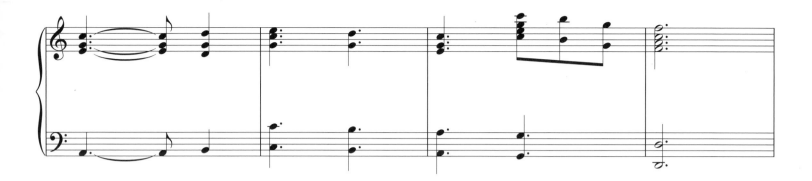

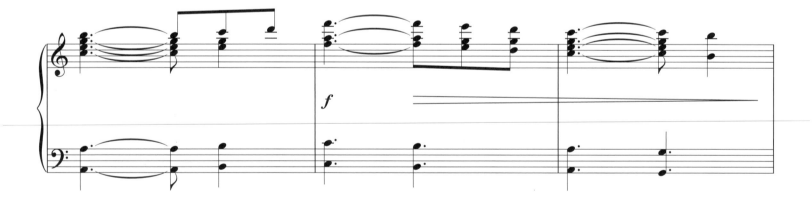

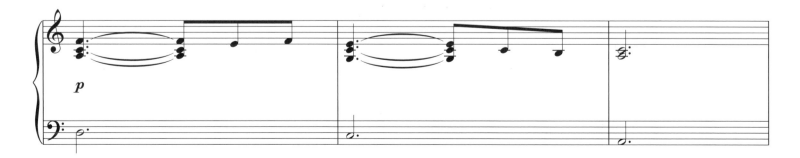

cresc.

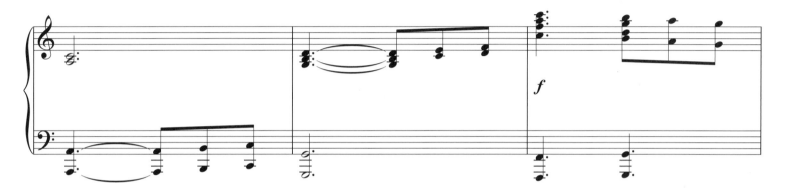

f

p

Beauty and the Beast

from *Beauty and the Beast*

Music by Alan Menken
Lyrics by Howard Ashman

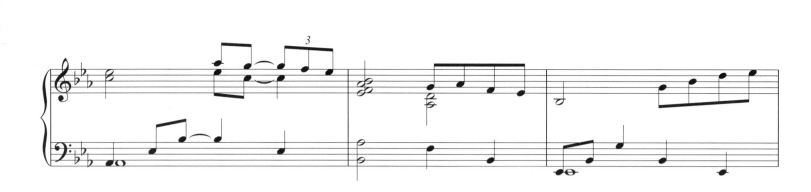

Big My Secret

from *The Piano*

By Michael Nyman

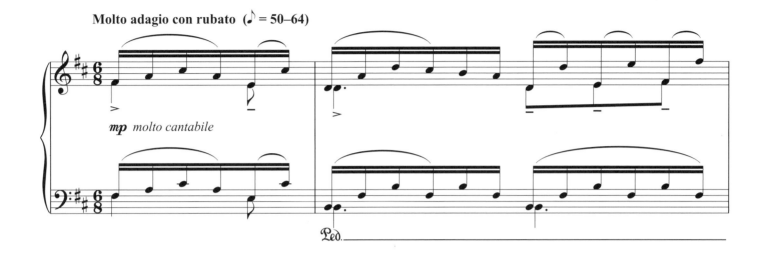

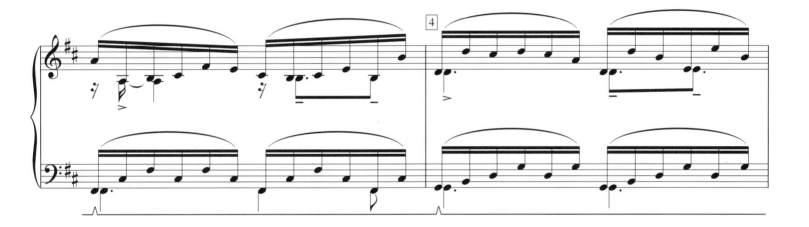

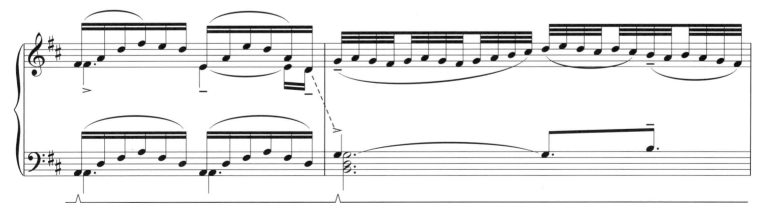

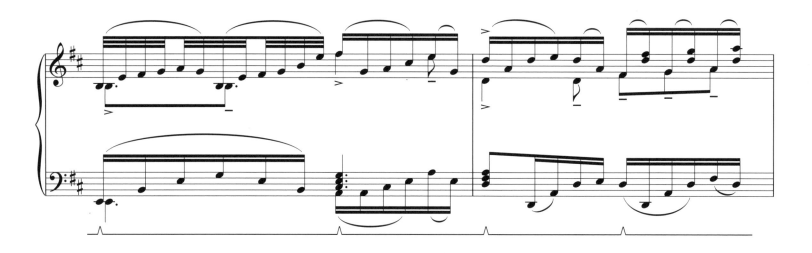

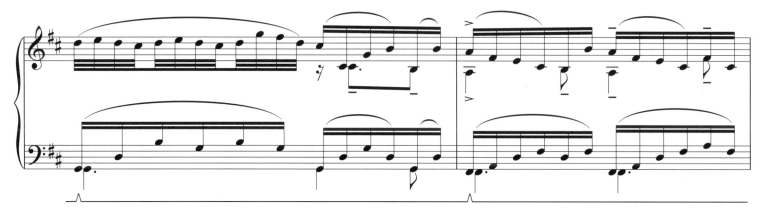

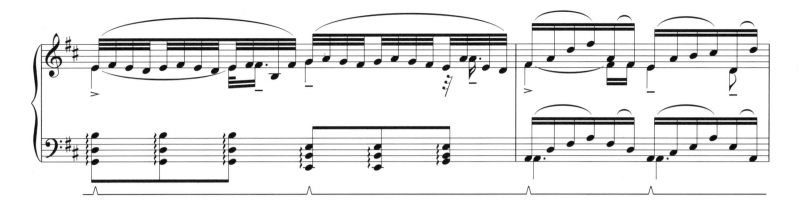

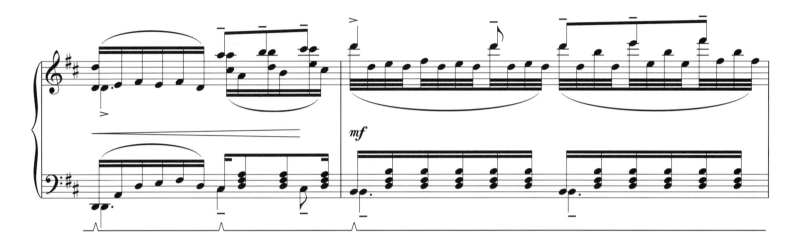

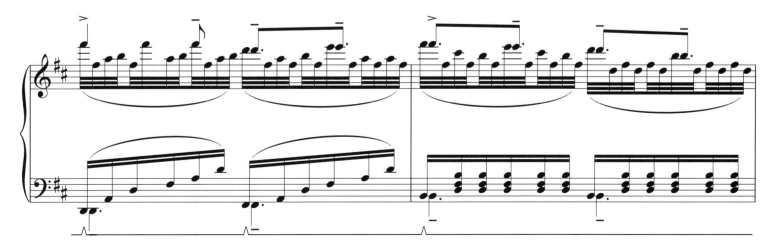

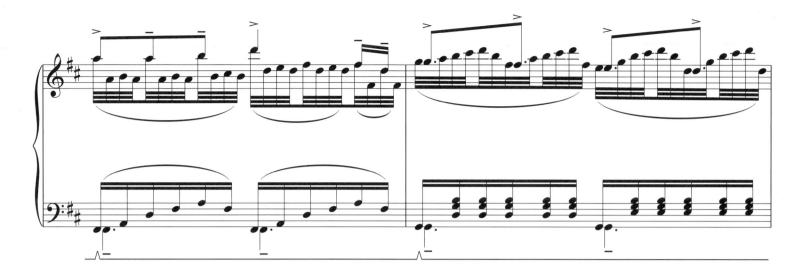

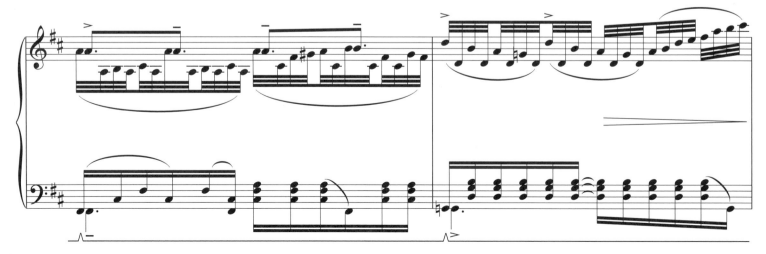

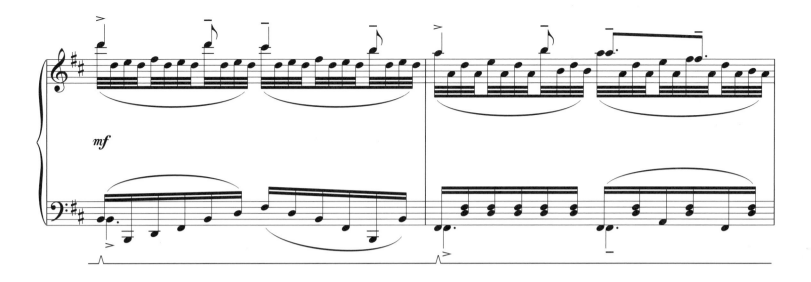

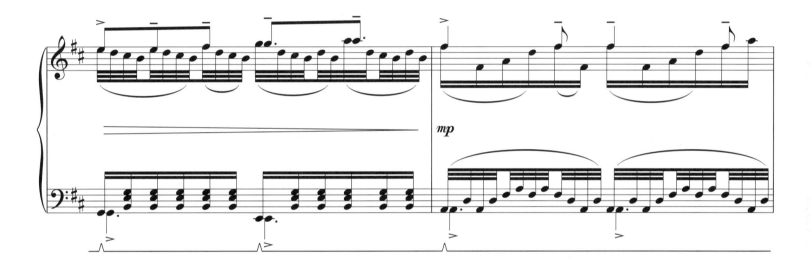

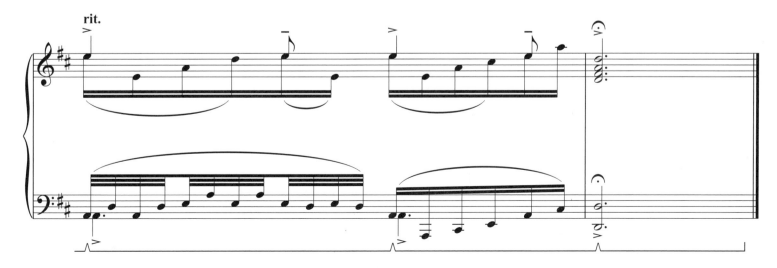

Cavatina

from the Universal Pictures and
EMI Films Presentation *The Deer Hunter*

By Stanley Myers

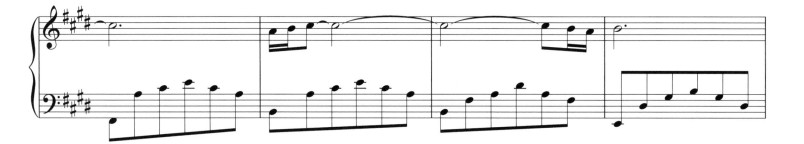

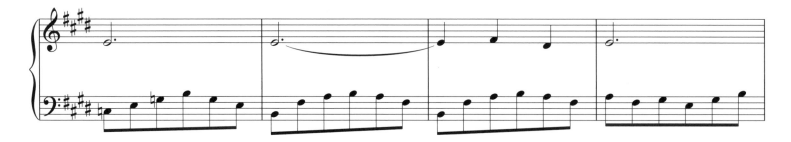

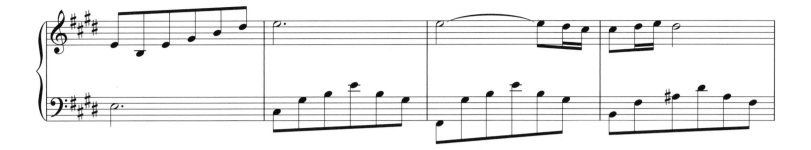

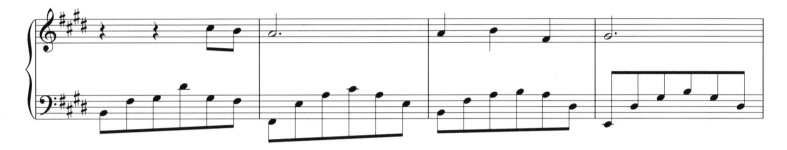

To Coda ⊕

cresc. poco a poco

cresc. poco a poco

D.C. al Coda

CODA

Comptine d'un autre été: L'après-midi

from *Amélie*

By Yann Tiersen

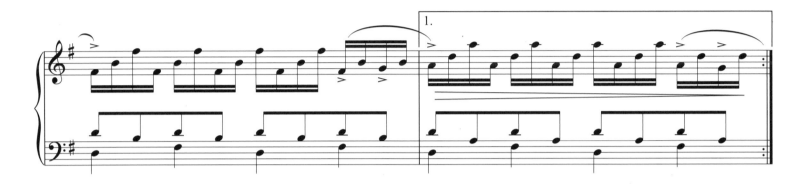

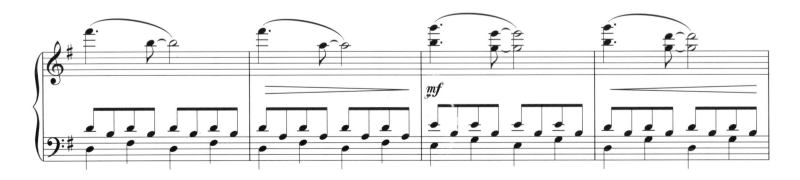

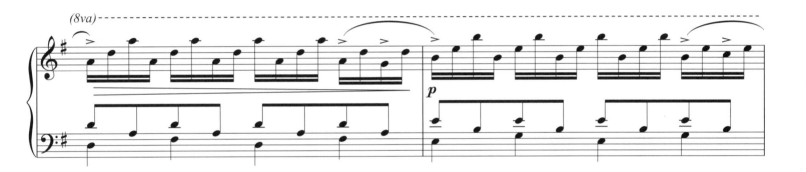

Cinema Paradiso

from *Cinema Paradiso*

By Ennio Morricone and Andrea Morricone

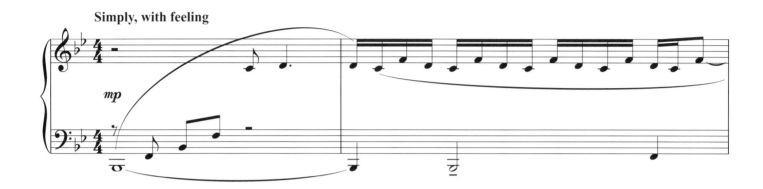

Dawn

from *Pride & Prejudice*

By Dario Marianelli

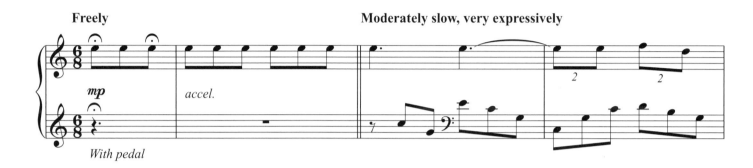

Moderately fast, with motion

29

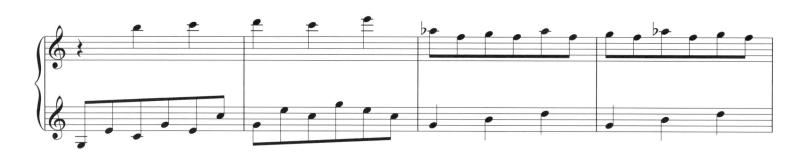

Slightly slower

Slowly

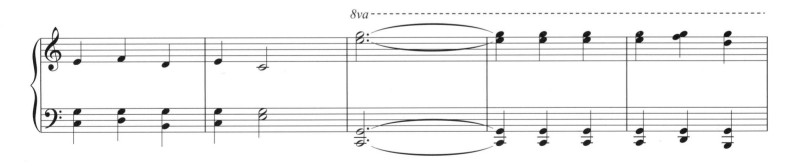

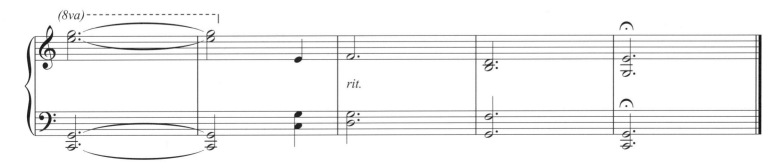

Downton Abbey Theme

from *Downton Abbey*

Music by John Lunn

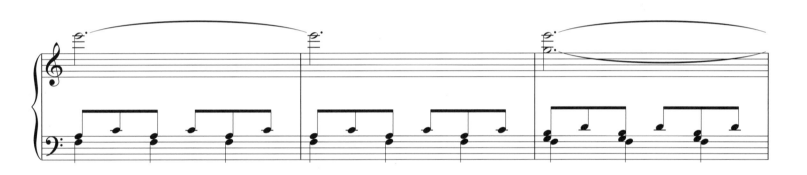

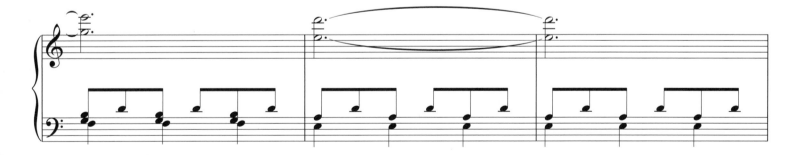

A Dream Is a Wish Your Heart Makes

from *Cinderella*

Music by Mack David and Al Hoffman
Lyrics by Jerry Livingston

Slower

arpeggio ad lib.

The Ellie Badge

from *Up*

By Michael Giacchino

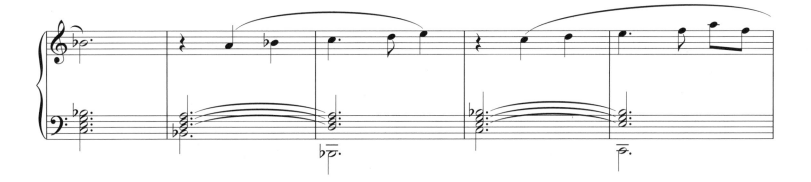

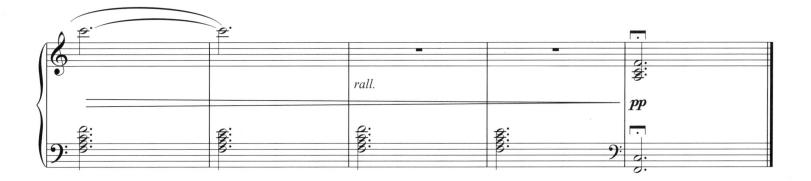

Escape!
from *The Hours*

By Philip Glass

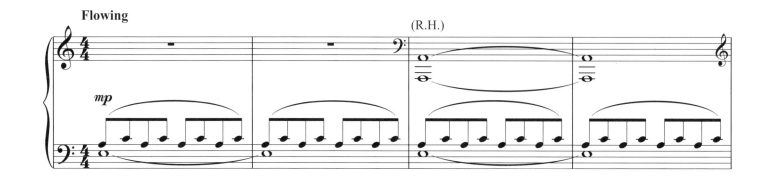

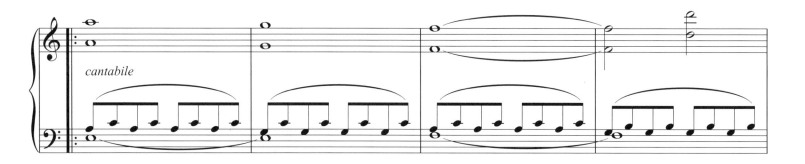

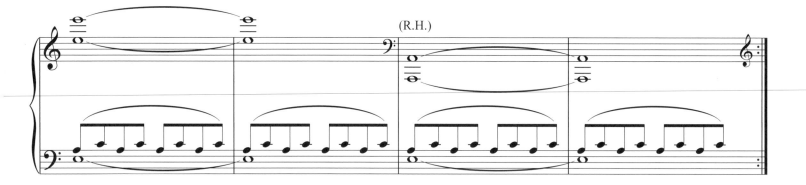

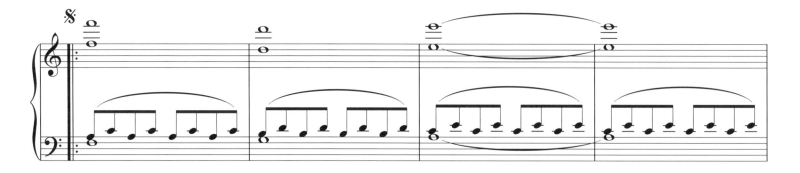

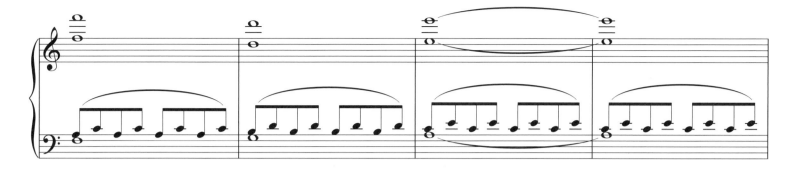

To Coda ⊕

(no repeat if following D.S.)

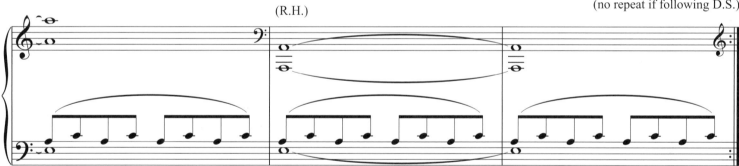

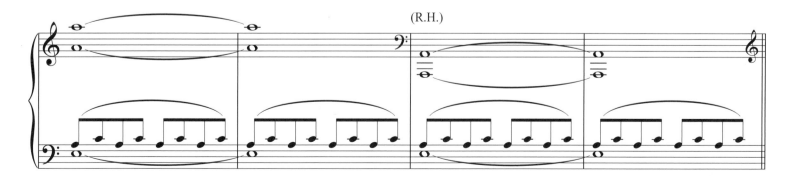

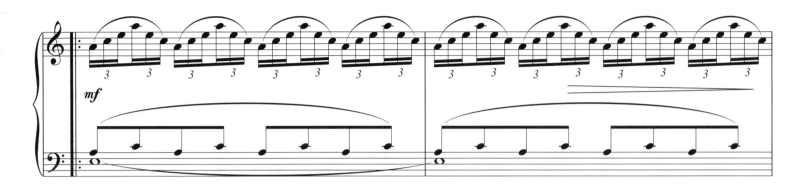

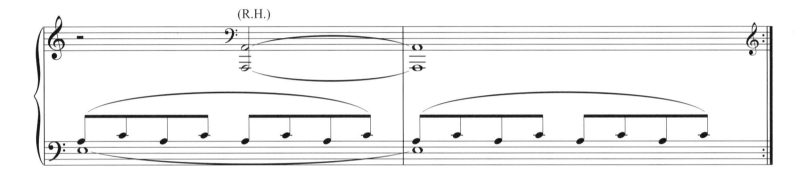

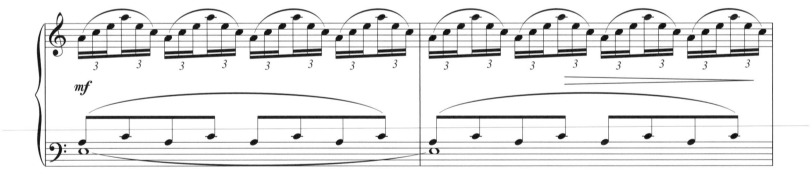

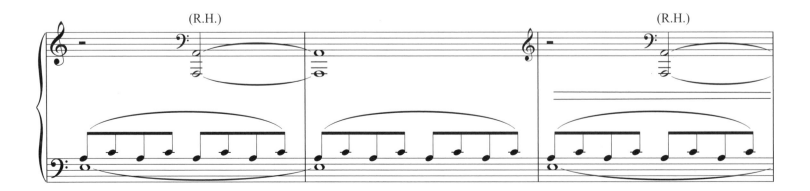

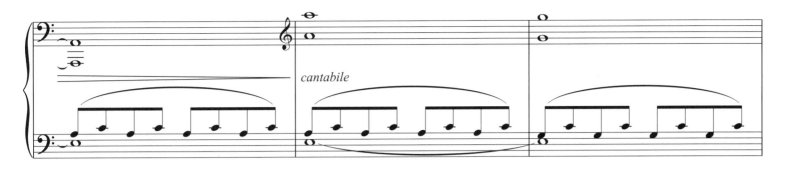

cantabile

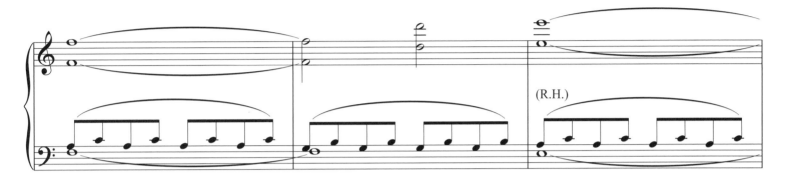

(R.H.)

D.S. al Coda

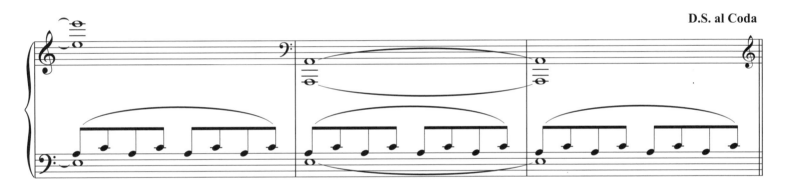

CODA

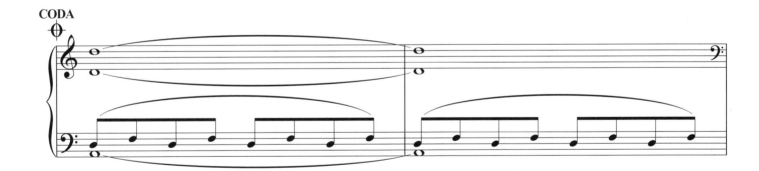

(R.H.)

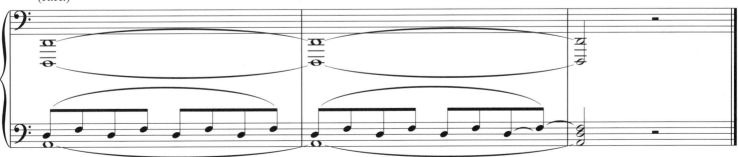

Feather Theme

from the Paramount Motion Picture *Forrest Gump*

Music by Alan Silvestri

(lightly)

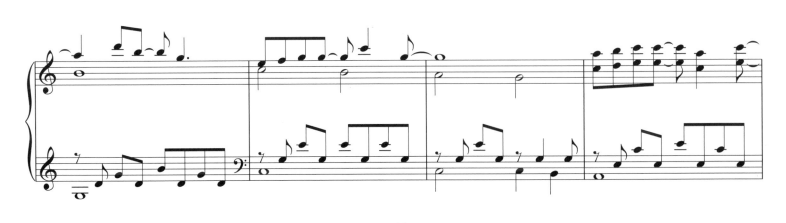

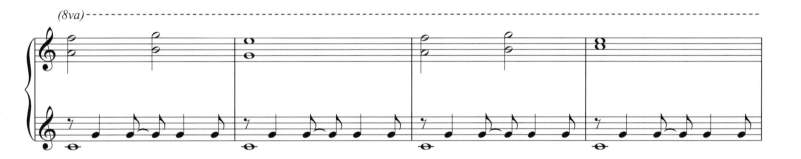

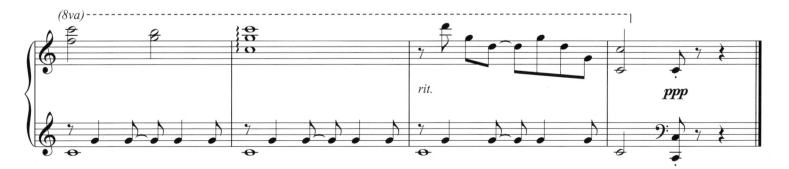

Fly

featured in *The Intouchables*

By Ludovico Einaudi

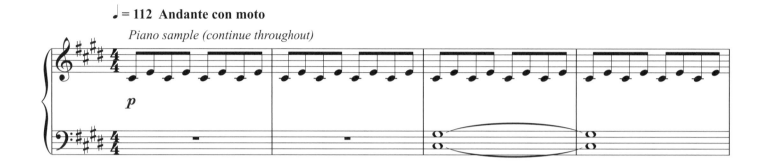

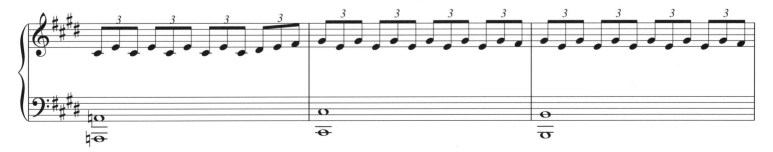

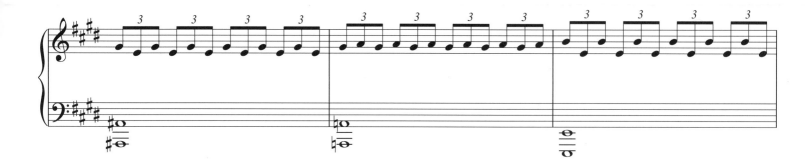

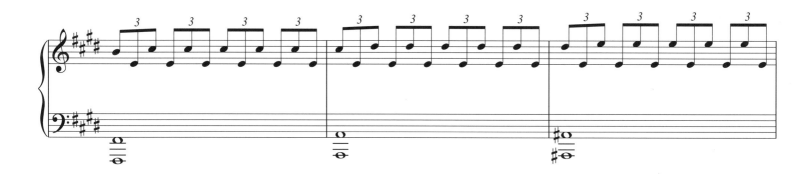

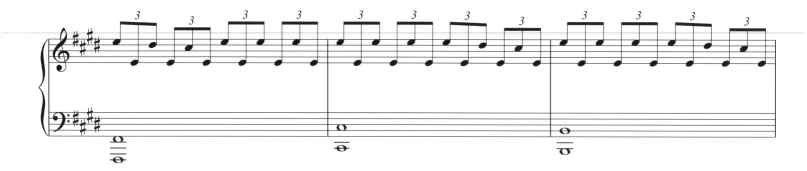

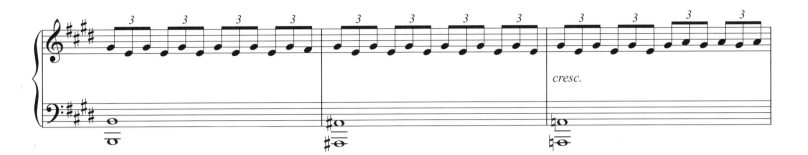

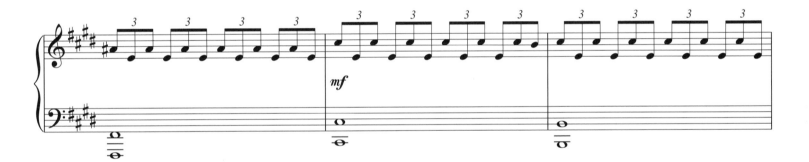

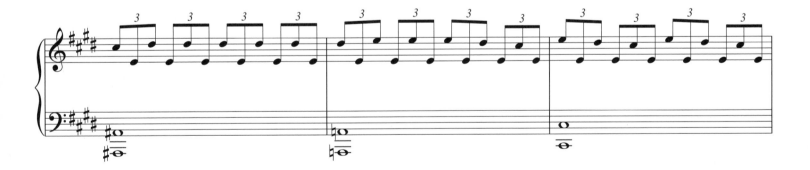

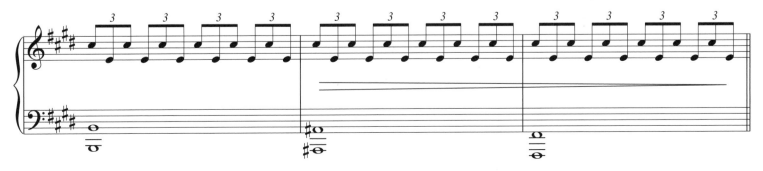

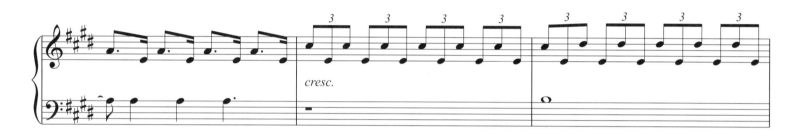

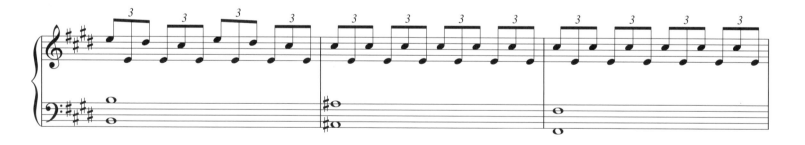

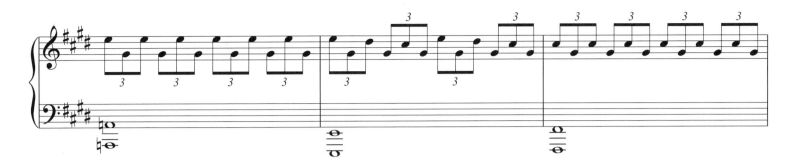

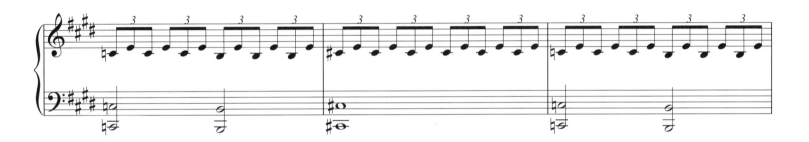

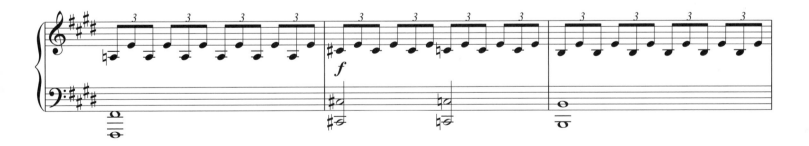

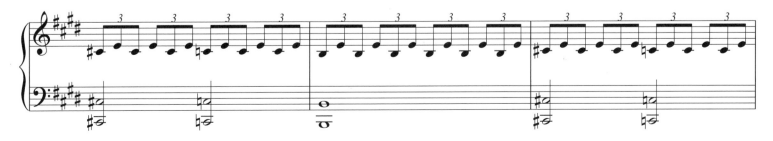

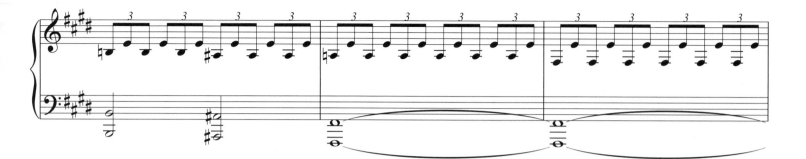

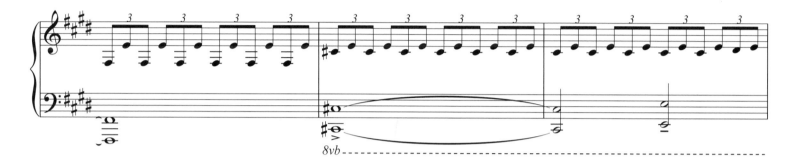

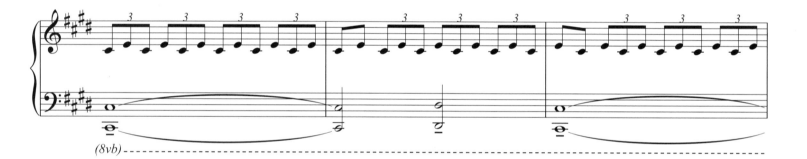

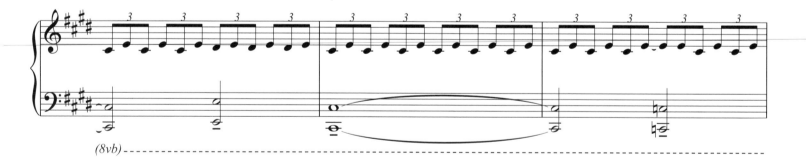

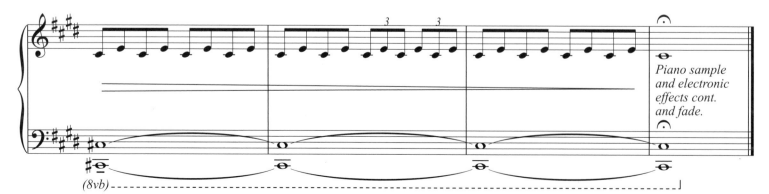

Piano sample and electronic effects cont. and fade.

Home

from *The Beauty Inside*

By Dustin O'Halloran

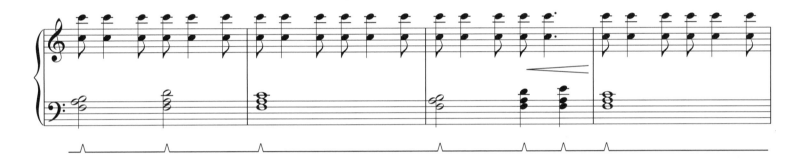

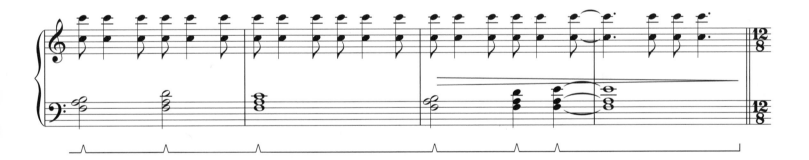

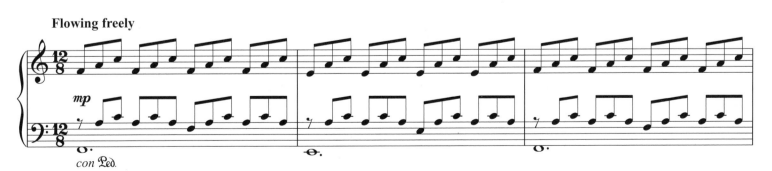

Ice Dance

from the Twentieth Century Fox Motion Picture
Edward Scissorhands

By Danny Elfman

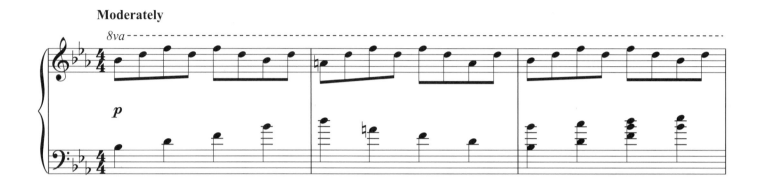

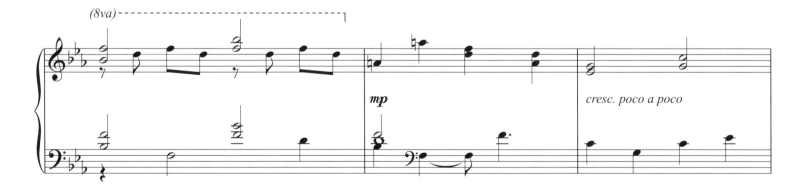

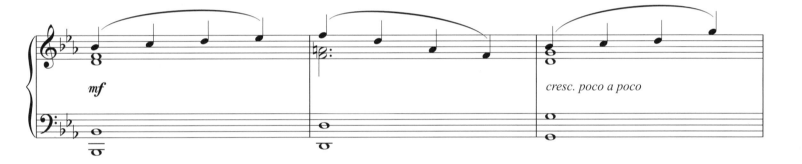

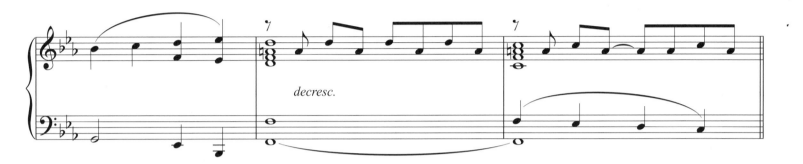

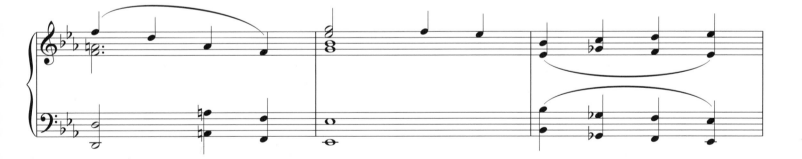

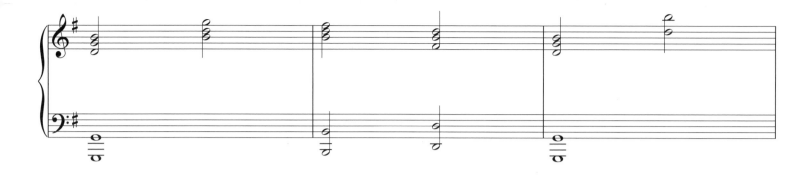

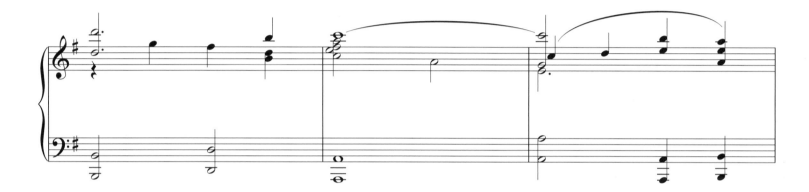

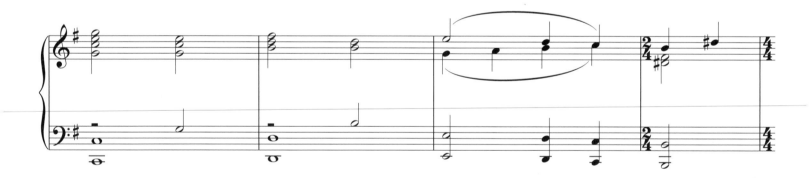

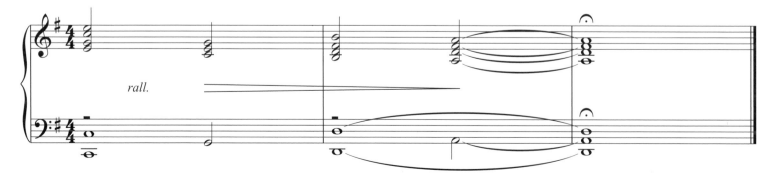

rall.

Il Postino (The Postman)

from *Il Postino*

Music by Luis Bacalov

Moderately

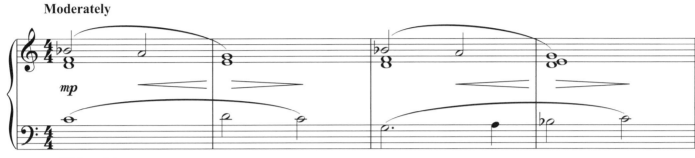

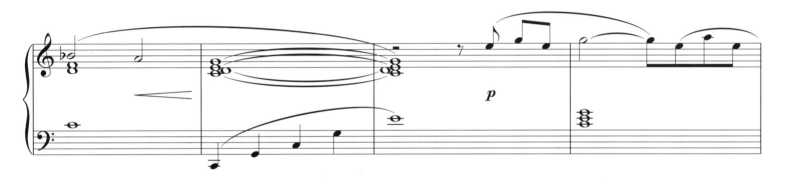

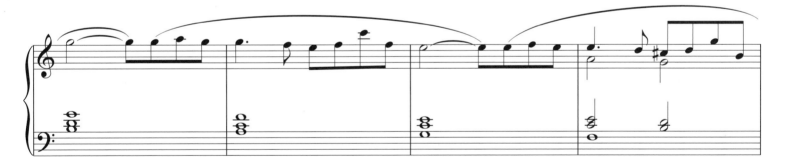

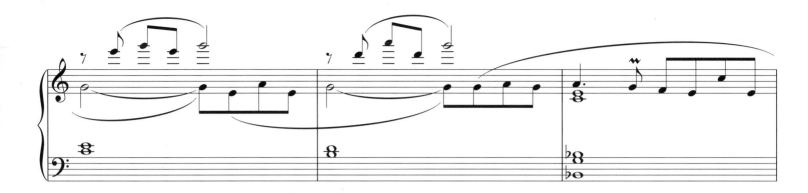

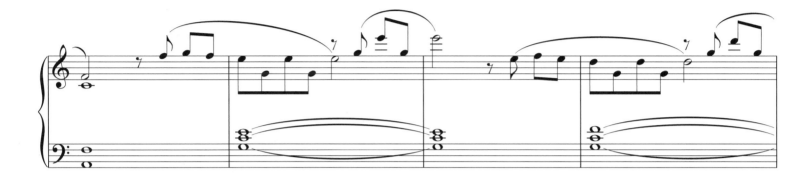

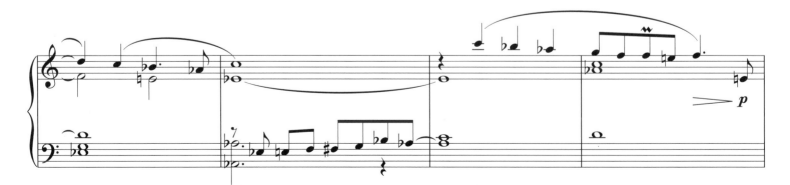

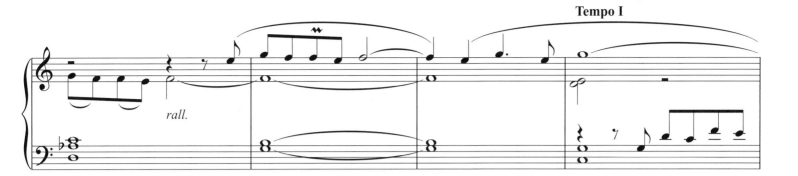

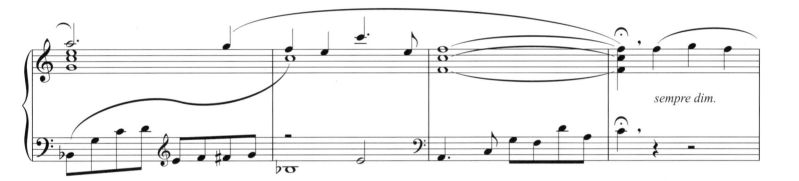

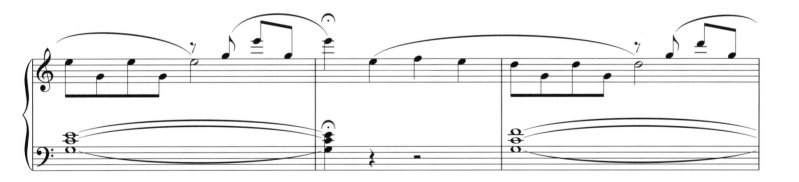

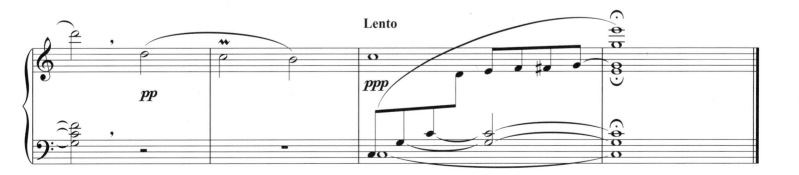

Lamentation for a Lost Life

from *Taboo* TV Series

Composed by Max Richter

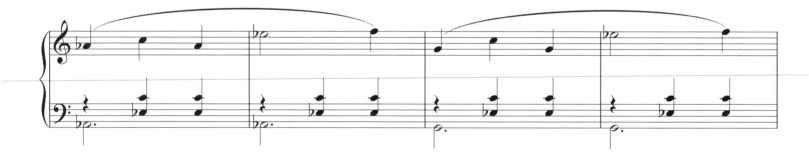

D.S. al Coda

CODA

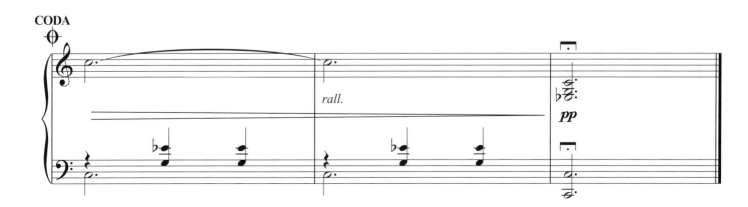

rall.

pp

Lion Theme

from *Lion*

By Dustin O'Halloran and Hauschka

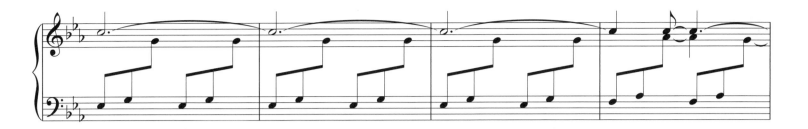

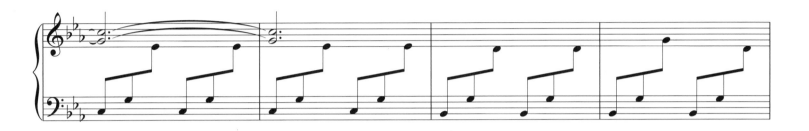

mf grandioso

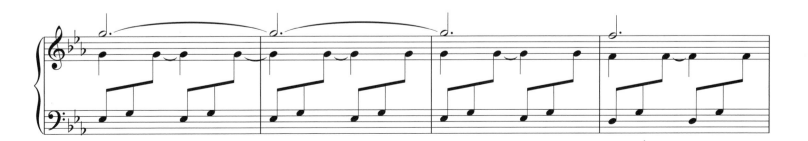

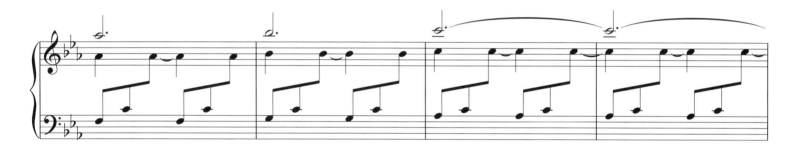

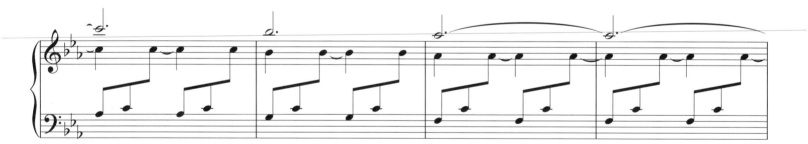

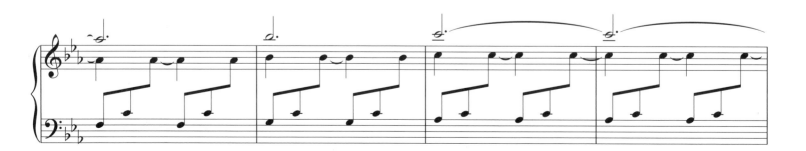

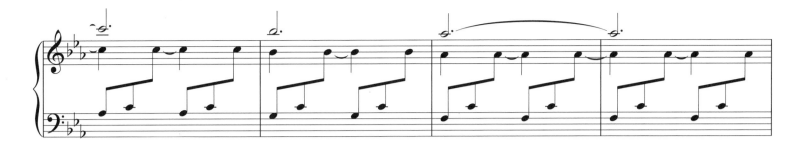

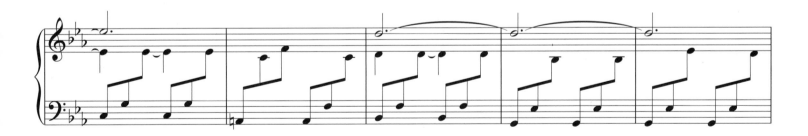

Love Theme

from the Paramount Picture *The Godfather*

By Nino Rota

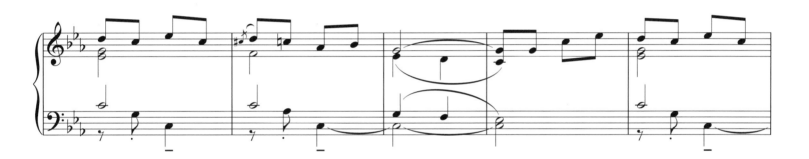

Light of the Seven

from the HBO Series *Game of Thrones*

By Ramin Djawadi

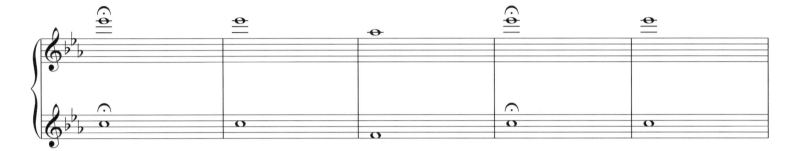

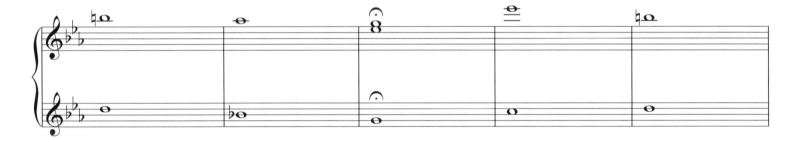

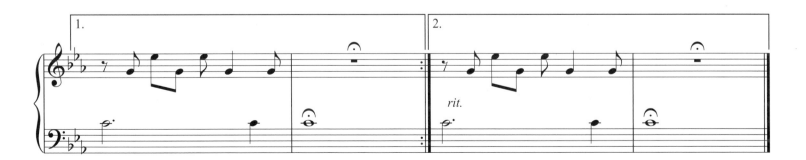

A Model of the Universe

from *The Theory of Everything*

By Jóhann Jóhannsson

Merry-Go-Round of Life

from *Howl's Moving Castle*

By Joe Hisaishi

$\quad\musEighth = 176$

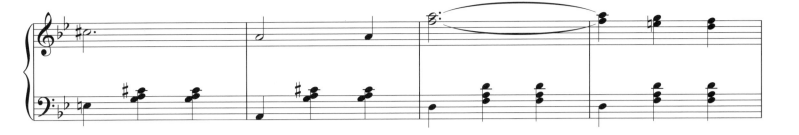

Moon River

from the Paramount Picture *Breakfast at Tiffany's*

Words by Johnny Mercer
Music by Henry Mancini

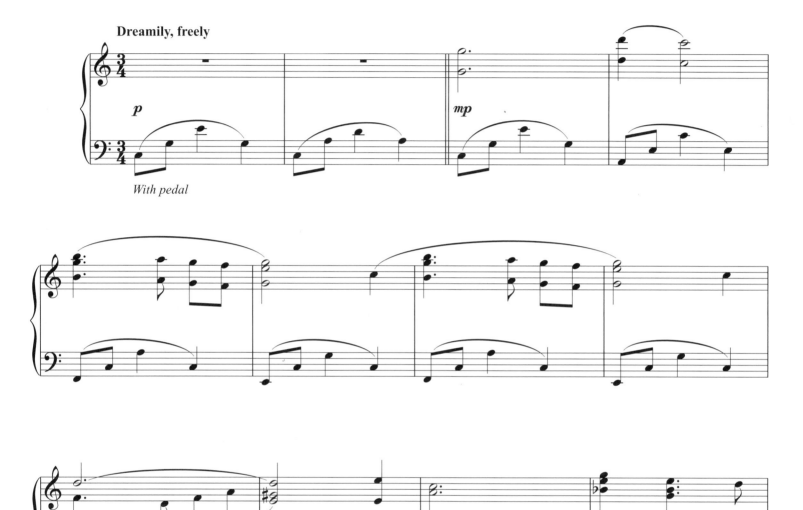

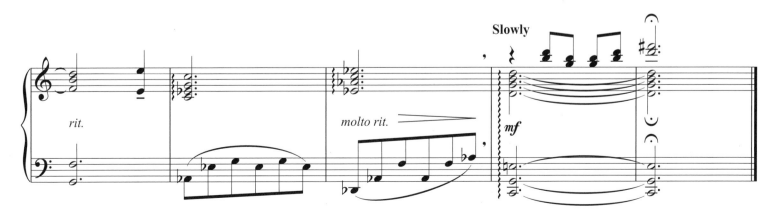

The Music of the Night

from *The Phantom of the Opera*

Music by Andrew Lloyd Webber
Lyrics by Charles Hart
Additional Lyrics by Richard Stilgoe

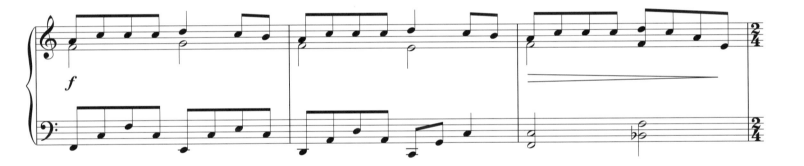

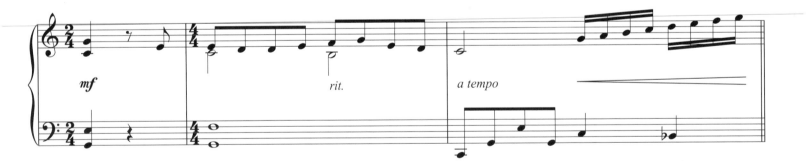

Tempo I

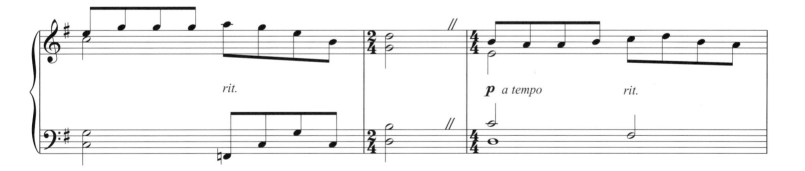

Pure Imagination

from *Willy Wonka and the Chocolate Factory*

Words and Music by Leslie Bricusse and Anthony Newley

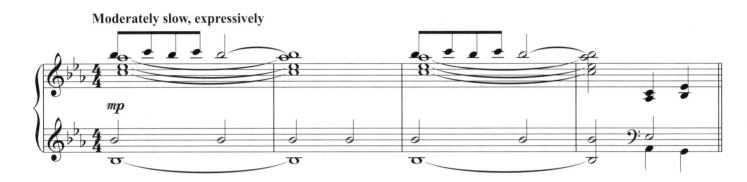

The Shape of Water

from *The Shape of Water*

By Alexandre Desplat

Smoothly

With pedal

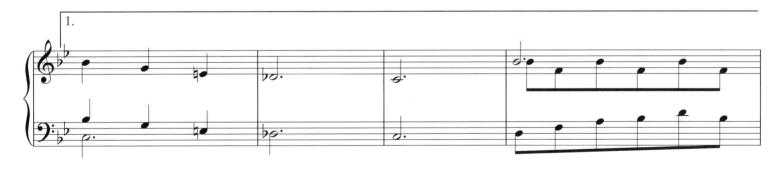

Somewhere in Time

from *Somewhere in Time*

By John Barry

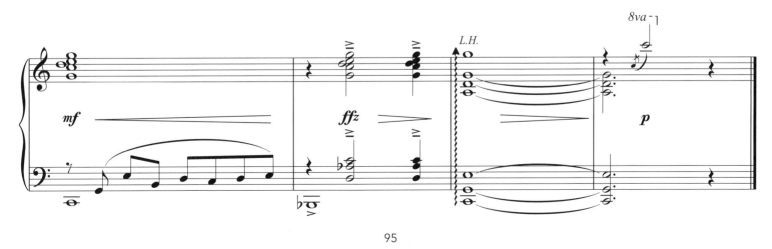

Theme from *Schindler's List*

from the Universal Motion Picture *Schindler's List*

Music by John Williams

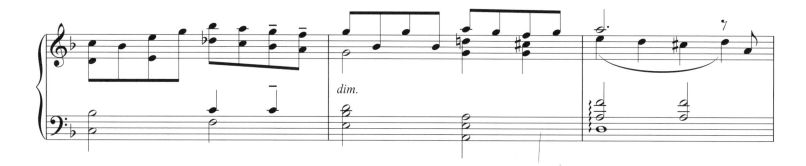

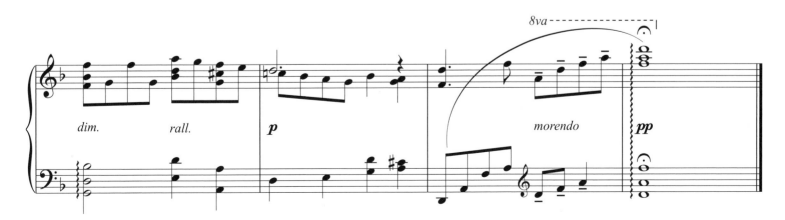

Together We Will Live Forever

from *The Fountain*

By Clint Mansell

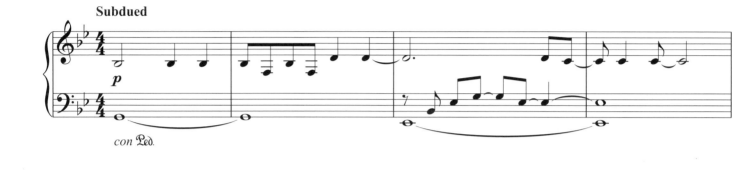

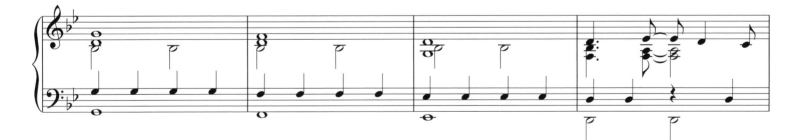

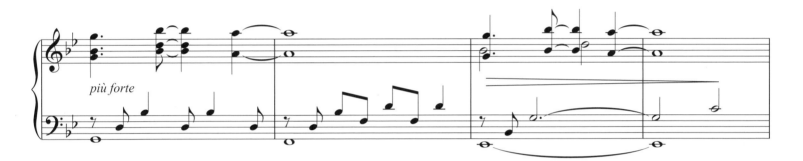

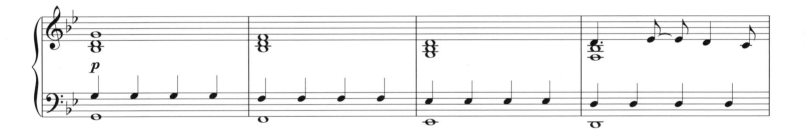

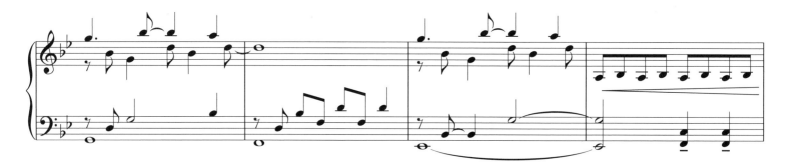

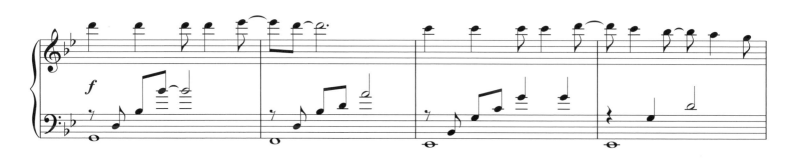

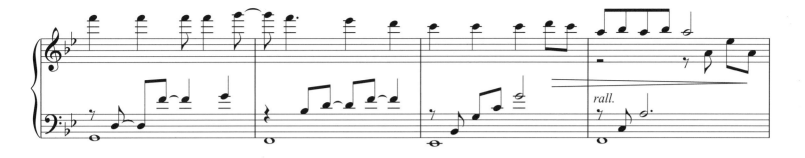

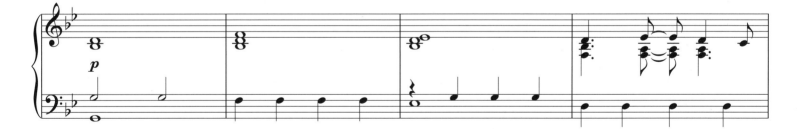

Discover the rest of the series...

ORDER No. HL00286009

ORDER No. HL00286428

ORDER No. HL00295379